Magdalen Bowyer

MAGICAL ARTS GODDESS INSPIRED

Vancouver, British Columbia
Canada

Love Is
By Magdalen Bowyer

Published by MAGI
Magical Arts Goddess Inspired
ISBN: 978-0-9938552-1-4

Illustrated by Joan Trinh Pham
Design & Layout by Lighthouse24

For Masa
a Rain of Blessings
for the DAM you
were Born!

for women

and the children of women

With love
MP

Love is a many-splendored thing . . . right?

So . . . how many times have you loved
or wanted to love someone
only to have them disappoint you?

Have you ever wondered
what's up with that?

What if you knew
it has nothing to do with them
and everything to do with you?

How would that change your life?

Could you take responsibility for yourself
without blaming yourself?

Would you learn what love
wants to teach you
about you?

Because there are no mistakes.

You draw into your life precisely the relationship that is perfect for you.

Every time. No exception.

Even when it feels awful.

You can turn awful
into awe-full
when you know there is
an Emotional Labyrinth
you must travel . . .
within you.

The path is strewn with stones
you will need to clear away.

The steps you take on this journey
compose the life you make and
you are always travelling now.

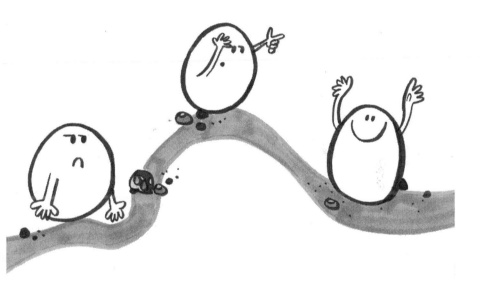

As you walk, you believe
you are looking for love.

And you believe this love you are seeking
will be found NOT in your inner world
where the path is travelled
but in the outer world
where you can see the other.

You will encounter dissatisfaction,
disappointment and disillusionment
which might cause you to wonder
why you are walking at all!

But the truth is
that you are looking for love
in all the wrong places.

The stones you stumble upon
will be feelings and you'll need to
learn what they mean for you.

Emotions like fear, doubt, worry, anxiety,
resentment, and depression are common.

You may encounter judgement, competition
or hostility. You might have moments
of sadness, guilt or shame.

These are survival stones.

And they will trip you up!

But they serve a purpose.

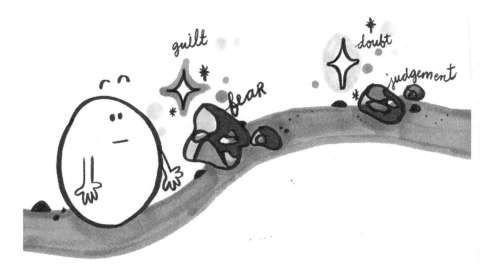

When feelings
get your attention,
you will have
a wonderful opportunity
to know yourself better.

Because you do not need
to get stuck in any of these
emotional experiences.

What feels like a rock
is only a block
until you get near it,
lift it, move it, and clear
your way forward.

Feelings will lead you through
storylines that live in you
but may not be yours.

How is this possible?

Well, you have inherited storylines
from your tribe – your family, society
and culture – and part of your job
as a human is to learn to discern
what IS you by learning
what is NOT you.

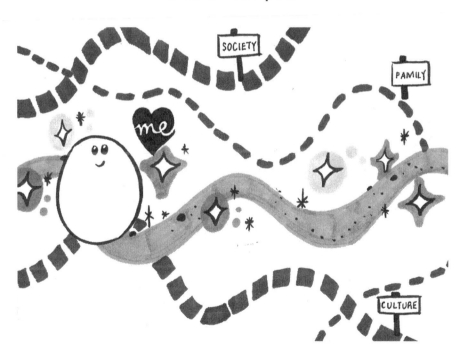

You will be satisfied enough
with these inherited storylines,
to live the part written for the character
you believe is you, until something happens
to shake your expectations about who you are
and what you are entitled to as deemed
by the story that is living you.

Then you will have cause to question the narrative.

It will feel like your world is falling apart.

But really, it is falling together.

Because storylines are only stories
that someone else has made up.

They are not the truth
of who you are.

This realization can be painful.

And it can also be liberating.

The pain is actually a friendly signal
that simply wants to bring you back home
to who you really are.

The emotional pain you feel
is an opportunity to broaden
what you think you are seeing,
sensing and perceiving
about who you are,
why you are here and
what you are doing.

Here in Earth School, you must
learn to master your human character
and your inherited storylines
so you may remember Me.

With Me, you can harness
your creative powers to serve the Life
that breathes your breath and beats your heart.

I demand you
become aware of the storylines
that have a hold on you,
awaken to their power, and
re-write your story
in your own voice
and in your own way
with Me.

Then every step you take
will bring you creative stones
that you can use
to hop, skip and jump
your way forward!

Who am I?

I am your divine feminine soul,
the balancing energy in union
with your sacred masculine.

The two are one. And the one is two.

Without Me there is no life.

I live in you.

And in every human being.

There are two things you need to know.

First, I can only do for you
what I can do through you.
This is the reason you must clear
the survival stones from your path.
It is the way
you break through
your inner boundaries
to activate and express
your soul gifts.
You are the first, the last
and the only you.
Earth School is where you
learn your wisdom and share Me.

Second, love is My essence.
So, the fact that you exist at all,
proves that love is alive.

Now, you must go forth
and show it to yourself –
that love is alive.

Get to know you
from the inside out
and you will know Me.

The only thing
you are ever meant to do
is get in Right Relationship
with Me.

I want to show you
how to step out of the stories
you no longer want to live in.

In Right Relationship with Me,
you will have access to
all you ever need.

I promise!

Do not look outside yourself
for what already lives within you.

And remember this:
no matter what pain you experience,
nothing has ever gone wrong.

You are simply walking the Labyrinth
in the way you are designed to do.

You and I are in this together.

If you allow me,
I will show you how
every being you encounter
brings you self-knowledge –
they hold a mirror for you.

Look through My eyes of love
and you will see yourself clearly.

There is a new story
that is wanting to be told
as your life.

You don't yet know the plot,
the character or the action
but I am here to teach you.

When we are in harmony,
you will feel the ease and fun of it
and that's the way it's meant to be.

No human being
will ever show up for you
the way I will.

I am your divinity.

You are designed
to create your life-story
through me.

When you let go
of the expectation that
somebody should love you
in some way,
and you invite Me to
radiate the love that is within you,
then something miraculous happens.

You turn inward and find something
you have been waiting so long for –
and it is right here within you!

So, be brave.

Be bold.

Be selfish.

Learn to romance Me.

I am
the dance of creation
wanting to move through you,
as you,
for you
and for all of life!

As your perception grows
and your inner boundaries soften,
you will better hear Me.

I am talking to you always.

You only need
to still yourself
and listen.

You will learn to trust Me
on this intimate journey.

Together we will find your voice.

And fuel the fire
of all you desire.

With your focus here
on Me,
you'll be empowered
to draw to yourself
all manner of magic
because now you have
what it takes
to love all people,
places and things
without condition.

You will finally understand
that love is not a force
to be objectified.

Love is the activity of your being.

Where you are, love is.

When you are aligned
with the truth
of who you and I
are together –
a divine creator –
the emotional landscape
of your experience
will change.

In joy,
you will be inspired
by ordinary things.

Peace will emanate from you.

You will know your own power.

And because you are drawing
these qualities from Me,
there is no limit
to the romance
we can enjoy!

When you have fallen
truly, madly and deeply
in love with Me,
you will radiate
a light so loving
that people cannot help
but love you.

You will seek nothing from them
because you are no longer
seeking love outside yourself.

Yet they will give you so much!

Because the love within them
is being drawn forth
through our Loving Presence.

When you are being love
then we will attract love
because now
you have learned
what love is.

I solve.

May this story
be an open portal
for Divine Mother's grace

Blessed Gratitude

I thank all my foremothers who prayed me into being.
I am grateful for my life. And I am devoted to
our evolution as fully human beings.

The Author – Magdalen Bowyer

The Illustrator – Joan Trinh Pham

Magdalen Bowyer was born and raised in Saskatchewan but she fell in love with the West Coast of Canada and has made it her home for more than two decades. Her love of writing always had her believe she would tell stories and make books. What she didn't foresee was the privilege bestowed upon her as a counsellor to women who entrust her with the intimate stories of their lives.

Through a lifetime of learning to love and trust herself, she is devoted to empowering women to re-member who we really are – wisdom, power and love in action. As women awaken to co-create intimate relationship with the Divine Feminine, we un-earth the truth that all power is Divine, flows from within and wants to be mobilized in our lives. Personal empowerment is the natural result when we align with the Divine and harness our real power. Then all of life rejoices in the creative blessings and innate compassion of woman as a mighty being in all her radiance.

This is her second book. You can find her at www.magdalen.ca

Joan Trinh Pham is an artist, modern palmist + hospice palliative care nurse. She loves to empower others to come alive with sparkly eyes for maximum enjoyment of their radically unique, juicy life paths. Joan enjoys sharing joy, beauty + magic through calligraphy + doodles. She frequently devises practical stratagems to radiate love primarily through the innovative modalities of hand analysis + death awareness education. Her work + creative adventures can be found at www.joantrinhpham.com

Made in the USA
Middletown, DE
01 August 2016